D1481830

Violence
on the
Screen

Clive Gifford

A+
Smart Apple Media

3 1267 13984 4649

First published in 2006 by Evans Brothers Limited
2A Portman Mansions, Chiltern Street, London W1U 6NR

Produced for Evans Brothers Limited by Monkey Puzzle Media Limited
Gissing's Farm, Fressingfield, Suffolk IP21 5SH, UK

This edition published under license from Evans Brothers Limited. All rights reserved.
Copyright © 2006 Evans Brothers

Editor: Cath Senker
Designer: Mayer Media Ltd.
Picture research: Sally Cole and Lynda Lines

Picture acknowledgements
Action Plus 28; Corbis 4 (J. Dickman), 5 (Reuters TV/IRIB), 6 (Alinari Archives), 7 (Bettmann),
9 (J. Woodcock), 15 (L. Addario), 19 (G. Mendel), 23 (B. Rondel); Alamy front cover (Richard
Osbourne/Blue Pearl Photographic); Empics 20 (M. Croft/PA); Getty Images 16 (The Image Bank/
Andy Bullock), 30 (AFP), 33 (AFP), 38 (R. Chapple), 39, 40 (Peter Cade), 41, 43 (J. Merriman);
PYMCA 11; Kobal 13 (Warner Brothers), 32; Rex Features 14 (Sipa Press), 17 (Sipa Press), 21 (Action
Press), 22 (Alix/ Phanie), 25 (A. Segre), 31, 34 (RS/Keystone), 36 (Sipa Press), 37 (20th Century
Fox/Everett); Reuters 5 (STR), 42 (R. Stubblebine); Ronald Grant Archive 10, 12, 26, 29; Topfoto 8, 18,
24, 27, 35 (Image Works/P. Hvizdak).

Published in the United States by Smart Apple Media
2140 Howard Drive West, North Mankato, Minnesota 56003

U.S. publication copyright © 2007 Smart Apple Media
International copyright reserved in all countries. No part of this book may
be reproduced in any form without written permission from the publisher.
Printed in China

Library of Congress Cataloging-in-Publication Data

Gifford, Clive.
Violence on the screen / by Clive Gifford.
p. cm. – (Voices)
Includes bibliographical references and index.
ISBN-13: 978-1-58340-985-5
1. Violence on television—Social aspects. I. Title. II. Voices (North Mankato, Minn.)
PN1992.8.V55G54 2006
303.6—dc22   2005057614

9 8 7 6 5 4 3 2 1

CONTENTS

SCREEN VIOLENCE

Violence takes many forms. It can sometimes be to animals or property. Frequently, it is against other people. Violence, and the threat of violence to scare people or force them to do something, is usually illegal.

No solution

Adam Yauch, of the rap group the Beastie Boys, is one of millions who believe that violence is never a solution:

" Being on either end of a violent situation, whether you seem to have come out with the upper hand or not, doesn't resolve anything. It escalates the problem. Hatred leads to more hatred. Violence leads to more violence. "

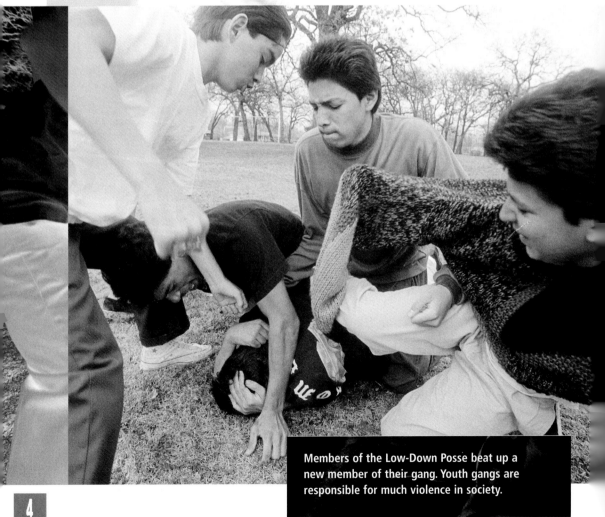

Members of the Low-Down Posse beat up a new member of their gang. Youth gangs are responsible for much violence in society.

Real-life violence is broadcast on TV. This image is from an Iranian broadcast of a train explosion that killed more than 200 people.

محمد ابراهیم سماواتی

خبرنگار آزاد صدا وسیمای مرکز خراسان

گفت : پنج هزارو ۹۰۰ نفرکارنظارت ، حفاظت و برگزاری انتخابات مجلس هفتم

Hot topic

Screen violence refers to violent acts shown on television. It also refers to the many other mass media that can communicate images via a screen: movies, computer games, videos and DVDs, and streaming images on the Internet. There is an important debate about whether screen violence can cause real-life violence or create other harmful effects on the public.

Ted Turner, the founder of the CNN television network, believes that:

"TV is the single most significant factor contributing to violence in America."

Evidence to a United States Congressional subcommittee, 1993.

NUMBER OF VICTIMS OF ASSAULT IN 2000

Different countries count violent crimes in different ways.
Assaults are one type of violent crime.

COUNTRY	ASSAULTS	TOTAL POPULATION (MID-2005)
Australia	141,124	20 million
UK	450, 865	60 million
U.S.	2,238,480	296 million
France	106,484	61 million
Canada	233,517	33 million

United Nations Survey of Crime Trends, 2002

IS THERE MORE VIOLENCE TODAY?

We do not have accurate statistics from the distant past, so it is hard to tell whether we live in a more or less violent world now. Yet we know that violence has existed in society since the dawn of humankind.

Ancient entertainment

Violence has been a common theme in books, art, and entertainment for thousands of years, as David, 15, from Manchester, England, comments:

" Violence has thrilled and excited people for centuries. Thousands of people used to come out to watch people being hanged or beheaded. There were violent sports such as bear baiting and savage mob football, while the ancient Romans had gladiators fight to the death. "

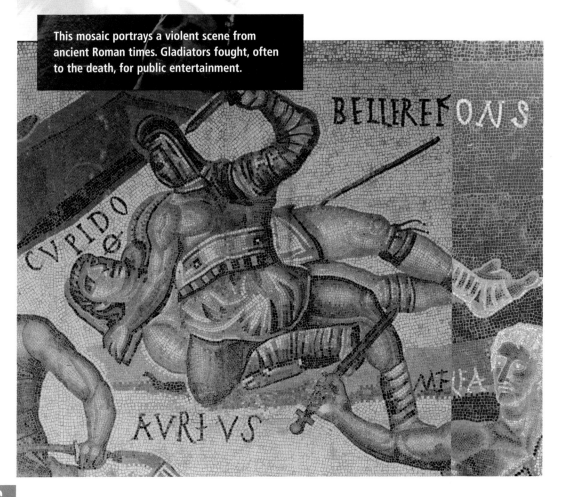

This mosaic portrays a violent scene from ancient Roman times. Gladiators fought, often to the death, for public entertainment.

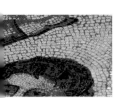

NUMBER OF HOUSEHOLDS WITH TV SETS IN THE U.S.

YEAR	NUMBER OF TV SETS	TOTAL POPULATION
1945	7,000	143.5 million
1950	3.8 million	151.3 million
1960	45.8 million	179.3 million
1970	59.5 million	203.2 million
1980	76.3 million	226.5 million
2004	106.9 million	293.0 million

An American family watches TV, 1953. The year before, the U.S. Congress held its first hearing about violence in films and TV programs.

While violence has been around for thousands of years, screen media, such as TV, movies, and computers, have a far shorter history. Few people had TV sets before 1950 or computers before the 1980s.

Beamed to your screen

Violent entertainment of the past was seen by relatively few people. Mass media, especially television and the Internet, allow violence to be beamed into millions of homes and watched every day. This is a key reason why many people, including Christian minister Kerby Anderson from Texas, are concerned about screen violence:

"Violence has always been a part of the human condition. But modern families are exposed to even more violence than previous generations because of the media. Any night of the week, the average viewer can see levels of violence approaching and even exceeding that of the Roman gladiator games."

Kerby Anderson, *Violence in Society*, 2002.

ARE CHILDREN AND TEENS MORE AT RISK?

Much of the debate about screen violence focuses on young people. They are considered more vulnerable to the possible harmful effects of viewing violence.

Under threat?

Young people watch a lot of TV, films, and videos and play computer games. They are still developing their view of the world and learning about right and wrong, which means they can be easily influenced. According to Jacob, 13, from Hamilton, New Zealand, this applies to teens as well:

" My classmates reckon they're no longer silly kids who copy cartoons. But I see them buying knives and brass knuckles they've watched being used in violent films. They're all getting into gangs just like in the videos. "

Children in war-torn Bosnia mimic what they have seen during the fighting. They use home-made guns to shoot at imaginary aircraft.

Three boys engage in play fighting in Britain. Can screen violence really prompt this behavior? Or are fighting and violence just a part of growing up?

WATCHING TV

Children in 23 countries surveyed watched an average of 3 hours of TV each day—50 percent more than the time spent on any other activity outside of school.

UNESCO, 1998

Watching and learning

Younger children often focus on the action in a violent scene without understanding the background to the violence and whether it is real or fantasy, good or bad. They can also learn by copying. Nisha, a 14-year-old girl from Leicester, England, recalls:

❝ My eight–year–old sister and I were watching a film that had a lot of ninja fighting in it, and all of a sudden, she leaped up and started kicking and hitting me for no reason! When my parents yelled at her, she just said, 'But the people on TV were doing it, and it looked fun!' ❞

"Screen images can play a big part in shaping children's understanding of the world."
National Society for the Prevention of Cruelty to Children (NSPCC), UK, 2003.

IS SCREEN VIOLENCE GLAMOROUS?

Fictional screen violence often appears dramatic and exciting. Many feel that the way violence is portrayed makes it seem glamorous.

Happy not horrific

Screen violence is often performed by the star of the show, frequently with the pain and suffering of the victims removed. As George Gerbner, founder of the Cultural Indicators Project in the U.S., states:

❝ **Most of the violence we have on television is what I call happy violence. It's swift, it's thrilling, it's cool, it's effective, it's painless, and it always leads to a happy ending.** ❞

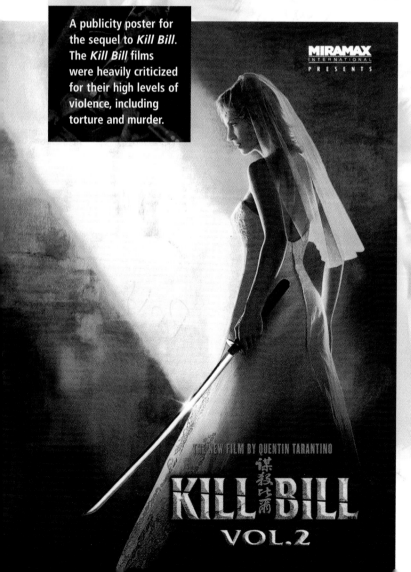

A publicity poster for the sequel to *Kill Bill*. The *Kill Bill* films were heavily criticized for their high levels of violence, including torture and murder.

MIRAMAX
INTERNATIONAL
PRESENTS

THE NEW FILM BY QUENTIN TARANTINO

KILL BILL
VOL.2

"Roughly half of TV violence involves no physical injury and no pain or suffering. Shows seldom depict long-term suffering of the victim and the negative impact on the family and community."

The National Television Survey, U.S., 1998.

A member of the Rolling 20s Bloods gang poses with an AK-47 assault rifle. Some movies, TV shows, and music videos glorify gang violence by making it appear glamorous to use weapons.

What about the victims?

Little attention is paid on-screen to the victims of violence. As Martin, an American teen victim describes, a violent attack can leave you physically and emotionally scarred:

" How often do you see a guy attacked in a film and then, moments later, he's fine, ready for more action? It's not like that. These two guys beat me. They broke my leg. I sobbed and shook for days. I was on crutches for six weeks. Even now, a year later, I get afraid to go out some days. **"**

VIOLENCE ON TV

In the largest-ever study of the content of TV programs, the National Television Violence Study (NTVS) analyzed nearly 10,000 hours of programming from 23 different cable and broadcast channels from 1994 to 1997.

They found that, of the violent acts shown on television:

58%   showed no pain

47%   showed no harm to victims

86%   featured no blood or gore

16%   showed long-term, realistic consequence of violence.

NTVS, U.S., 1998

IS SCREEN VIOLENCE ONLY MAKE-BELIEVE?

Some screen violence is real, but the majority is not. It is fictional violence acted out in cartoons, action movies, dramas, and soap operas, as well as video games. Does the fact that it is not real make a difference to viewers?

Hard to tell?

Some screen violence, such as space battles and cartoons, may appear obviously fictional to adults and teens but not always to younger children. Yet scenes of violence made using special effects or in a show that seems like real life, such as a gritty police drama, can look disturbingly realistic. Mansoor, a teen from Birmingham, England, is more concerned about lifelike violence:

❝ When Bruce Willis blows away a bunch of villains, it's funny. You know it's not real. I think violence in [British soap opera] EastEnders and other soaps is more shocking because it's more like real life. It's not silly or glossy. ❞

Targeted at children, some Looney Tunes cartoons in the 1970s were edited to cut out certain violent scenes.

DAFFY DUCK & ELMER FUDD IN "WISE QUACKERS"

A Looney Tune CARTOON IN TECHNICOLOR

A nightmare vision

Screen content is designed to stimulate your emotions. People may know that the violence they are watching isn't real, but it can still disturb them greatly, as Izzie, 13, from the UK, discovered:

❝ I have an overactive imagination, which means I can't watch scary films. My friends forced me to watch *The Shining*, and sometimes I still have trouble sleeping because I get so scared. ❞

Scenes from the 1980 horror film *The Shining*. The film featured violence and violent threats.

"Six to nine year olds generally still find it difficult to tell the difference between fantasy and reality. [They] may see cartoon characters as fantasy and laugh, but may also think that the message 'violence wins' is acceptable."
NSPCC Screen Violence pamphlet, 2002.

WHAT ABOUT REAL-LIFE VIOLENCE?

Real-life incidents of violence are shown in news footage, documentaries, and some sports broadcasts. Are these harmful or useful?

A homeless boy is moved on by a Brazilian policeman. Images of others' suffering can move people to try to help.

Right to know

Many news broadcasters and documentary filmmakers insist that the public has a right to know about events, even if they are unpleasant. Broadcasting graphic scenes of violence, war, and the suffering of victims may upset and shock, but it can lead to good actions. Flo, a teen from a suburb of Paris, France, describes how this happened to her:

" People need to know. It may shock them, but so what, compared to what the victims are suffering.... I cried when I watched how street children were beaten and abused. The next day, I did something about it and joined a charity. We may be saving lives because of what we saw on TV. "

Iraqi women grieve over the remains of bodies discovered in a mass grave. Are these images really necessary to tell the story, or do they just shock and upset people?

Disturbing effects

Some critics claim that news is made more violent and gory than it needs to be. Violent scenes can disturb some people or make them think the world is a more dangerous place (see pages 16–17). The guidelines for the British TV station the BBC indicate that violence can also make people care less:

❝ There is a balance to be struck between the demands of truth and the danger of desensitizing the audience. With some news stories, a sense of shock is part of a full understanding of what has happened. But the more often viewers are shocked, the more it will take to shock them. ❞

"So long as [violence] exists in society and the world, television programs must be able to reflect it, portray it, and report it."
Ofcom, British Office of Communications, 2003.

WHAT IS MEAN WORLD SYNDROME?

People who regularly view screen violence, whether it is real or not, may feel that the world is a more dangerous place than it actually is. This feeling is known as "mean world syndrome."

Young and old

"Mean world syndrome" can particularly affect the young and the elderly. Mirza lives in a wealthy, low-crime suburb of Toronto, Canada, but she is fearful:

" I have never been attacked or robbed here. But I think I am one of the lucky few. Youths are more violent now. I see it on the news every day. I'm 73 and won't go out now. I spent over $3,500 on bars, shutters, and an alarm system. **"**

Many elderly people, especially in large towns and cities, have an exaggerated fear of the world outside.

A vicious circle

Those who fear a violent world are likely to be suspicious of people and aim to protect themselves. They may also turn to violence more readily because they feel that they are likely to be attacked. Cardy, a Spanish teen, believes this can create a vicious circle:

> **"** I need to have a gun to protect myself, and I need to protect myself because I'm scared of something. But if you cared less about your security and more about people, then people wouldn't kill as much, and therefore you wouldn't have to have a gun to protect yourself. **"**

A young girl is instructed how to fire a handgun at the Front Sight Firearms Training Institute in Las Vegas. There are approximately 80 million gun owners in the U.S.

TV VIOLENCE

In 205 films shown in 2003 on Britain's five regular channels, there were:

1,121 incidents involving firearms

765 violent assaults

103 incidents of arson or explosives

277 incidents with knives and other offensive weapons.

Promoting a Culture of Violence 3—Mediawatch, 2004

Swearing in movies, music videos, and TV dramas is commonplace, and many people, through hearing the words all the time, are no longer shocked. Can the same thing occur with screen violence?

Less sensitive

Many think that young people can become desensitized by watching violence regularly—they are exposed to it so much that they care less about it, and the violence no longer shocks them. American psychologist Patricia Groessl believes this is the case:

❝ Children become less sensitive to the pain and suffering of others if they watch a lot of violent TV. They're more likely to behave in an aggressive or harmful way toward others. Children are watching long hours of violent TV and then identifying with the aggressors. ❞

Two men enjoy a violent gun-shooting video game in a New York arcade.

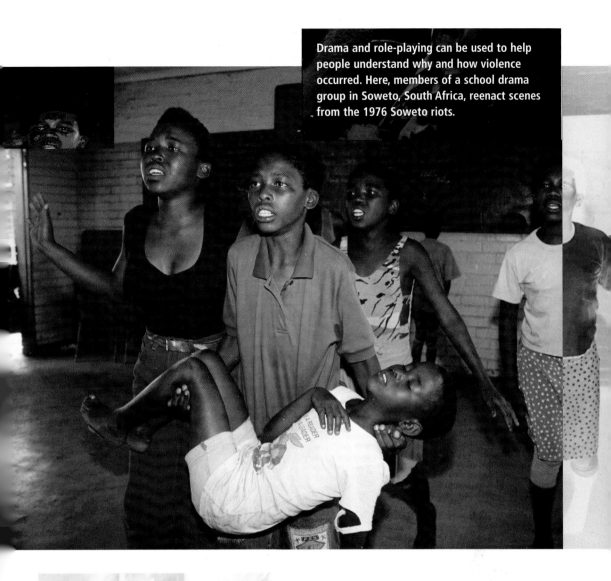

Drama and role-playing can be used to help people understand why and how violence occurred. Here, members of a school drama group in Soweto, South Africa, reenact scenes from the 1976 Soweto riots.

"Violence is like the nicotine in cigarettes. The reason why the media has to pump ever more violence into us is because we've built up a tolerance. In order to get the same high, we need ever-higher levels."
Lieutenant-Colonel David Grossman, psychology professor, *The Arizona Republic*, May 27, 1999.

Still shocked

Ralf is a 13-year-old Danish boy who believes that just because you watch violent imagery doesn't mean that you stop caring:

❝ I used to be scared a lot by violent media, but since I started taking acting lessons, I realize that it is all just faked. Sure, I like to watch violent and scary shows now. But I don't think I cannot feel or care. It can still shock me. It's just that I can handle it better now. ❞

CAN SCREEN VIOLENCE CAUSE REAL VIOLENCE?

Many researchers believe that people who view large amounts of screen violence are more likely to use violence in the real world.

The murder of 2-year-old Jamie Bulger (in photo) by two 10-year-old boys in 1993 prompted great debate in the UK on links between screen violence and real-life violence.

Causing aggression

Since the late 1960s, there have been many studies of screen violence and its effects on people. A number of these studies have found that people who watch violence regularly tend to be more aggressive and more likely to use violence themselves. Dr. Leonard Eron, chair of the American Psychological Association, believes:

❝ There can no longer be any doubt that heavy exposure to televised violence is one of the causes of aggressive behavior, crime, and violence in society. The evidence comes from both the laboratory and real-life studies. ❞

Seeing it in action

Craig, 14, lives in New South Wales, Australia, and has friends who are into violent movies and who have used violence themselves. He believes there is a link:

❝ I see that the more violent stuff you watch, the more edgy and angry it makes you. It gives you ideas for carrying things out. You see that fighting solves problems in films. When your life is mixed up and you have problems, you're gonna see fighting and violence as a way of sorting them out. ❞

Some people also point to the amount of advertising that funds commercial television stations. Why would advertisers spend millions if they did not think that TV had the power to influence people?

A student at a New York school is checked for weapons. According to the Bureau of Justice Statistics, in 2003, seven to nine percent of students in the U.S. reported being threatened or injured with a weapon at school.

"Viewing entertainment violence can lead to an increase in aggressive attitudes, values, and behavior, particularly in children. Its effects are measurable and long lasting."

Joint Statement on the Impact of Entertainment Violence on Children, 2000 (AHA, AAP, APA, AAFP, AACAP—psychology, psychiatric, and medical associations).

DOES VIOLENCE HAVE OTHER CAUSES?

Critics of the view that screen violence causes real-life violence point to the fact that the studies do not provide complete proof. They note that violence occurred long before TVs and computers were invented.

A violent teenager mugs a passer-by. The motivation for many acts of violence is to gain money or goods.

One rule for all?

If screen violence causes violent behavior, wouldn't a far greater proportion of the millions who watch violent programs attack people in real life? Min, a teen from High Wycombe, England, wonders about this:

" Loads of people watch violent programs and don't act on it at all. I think that it depends on the person's state of mind. If they take in what they watch and use it badly, then it's their fault. "

> "Violence on the screens, however loathsome, does not make a significant contribution to violence on the streets. Images don't spill blood. Rage, equipped with guns, does. Desperation does.... The drug trade does, poverty does."
>
> Todd Gitlin, *The American Prospect* magazine, 1994.

Not the key cause

People can be influenced to use violence by friends or bullies—or, if they are in a gang, by other gang members. They may commit violent acts to protect themselves, to gain a feeling of power, or to make money. Sarah, 16, from California, believes blaming screen violence is ridiculous when there are far more likely causes:

❝ This is ludicrous! What about a link between child abuse and poverty, and youth gang involvement and violent crime? I guess people who blame screen violence think that watching a gun-heavy movie like *The Matrix* will push more kids to violence than a poor, neglectful, or abusive household will. ❞

A victim of domestic violence shields herself. Children may experience domestic violence, and as a result, some may use violence as adults.

ARE COMPUTER GAMES A PROBLEM?

Computer graphics are now so advanced that the violent action in games is extremely lifelike. Are computer games simply a source of entertainment, or are they a major cause of aggression?

Letting off steam

Many players see violent computer games as merely fantasy and fun that has nothing to do with real life. Ben, 13, from Leicester, England, says:

" I play computer games all the time. It doesn't make me violent in real life—it helps me take out anger and stress in a controlled way. Games can also be social if you play with other people online. "

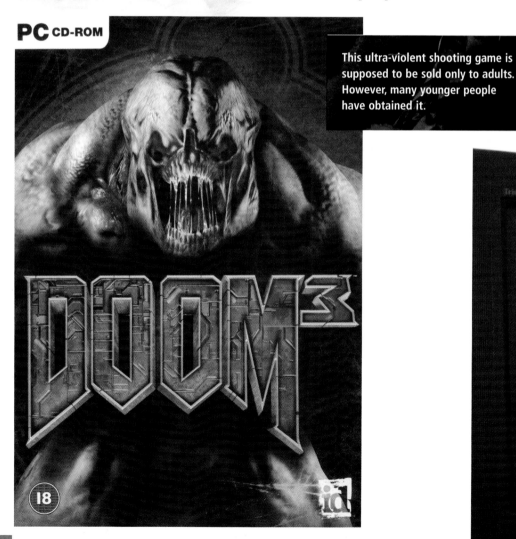

PC CD-ROM

This ultra-violent shooting game is supposed to be sold only to adults. However, many younger people have obtained it.

Different and worse?

Unlike films and TV, the game player has an active role. He or she is in control of the violence and can only progress by performing more and more violent acts. According to Danielle, 15, from Oregon, who has campaigned against violent video games:

❝ If you watch someone play a video game, they get excited. They want to win and get the points, and I don't think you should get that kind of excitement from killing. What do 'games' that let kids use a weapon to splatter blood teach? What do 'games' that give kids more points for headshots teach? ❞

"You're not just watching a movie, you're in the movie…. You're actually pulling the trigger. Getting killed is a drag because suddenly the game stops, and the only way to remain master of this intoxicating new universe is to kill."
Paul Keegan, reporter, *The Guardian*, Britain, 1999.

A six-year-old boy plays *Grand Theft Auto*, a violent and graphic computer game designed for adults only.

IS COPYCAT VIOLENCE COMMON?

Copycat violence is the carrying out of violence directly inspired by violent acts performed by someone else. This can include copying both fictional and real-life violence.

A rare phenomenon

Many researchers think that instances of serious copycat violence are rare and that there are far more common reasons for violence breaking out. Maddie, 15, from Surrey, England, is not convinced that copycat violence is a common act:

"Many of the violent kids who are caught, or their parents, claim it was because of this violent movie or that violent game, but is that really the case? Surely this is just an excuse, and really the kids' own mind and actions are to blame."

In 1994, Nathan Martinez from the U.S. shot and killed two members of his family after repeatedly watching the movie *Natural Born Killers* (which contains more than 50 murders) and dressing like the main character, Mickey Knox.

Two eight-year-old boys try out their martial arts skills in an interactive computer game called *Combatica*.

"The role of screen violence is to reinforce preexisting tendencies. Unlike ordinary teenagers, violent offenders seek out violent films and videos to reinforce and validate their own violent impulses. "
The British Board of Film Censors, 1998.

Mimicking murder

Incidents of copycat violence have been reported around the globe. In 2004, a French teen, obsessed with the horror film *Scream*, carried out a stabbing crime similar to one in the film. He was wearing a *Scream* mask. Travis, 14, from Caloundra, Australia, believes that copycat violence is relatively common:

" Copycat violence occurs. As kids, we copied World Wrestling Federation wrestling moves even when they hurt. Some people with serious problems may be searching for a way to commit violence. Clever and powerful movie plots and games could give them the techniques and inspiration they need. "

RIGHT TO FIGHT?

TV and films often portray a hero as one who solves problems with his or her fists, weapons, or some other form of violence. Does this send out the signal that it is right to fight?

Violence erupts during a Rugby League game. Professional athletes are important role models for many children who may try to copy their behavior, both good and bad.

Influential role models

The Center for Media and Public Affairs in Washington, D.C., estimates that more than 40 percent of violent acts in music videos, movies, and TV are performed by the good characters. There is often violence in sports, too. Critics of screen violence fear that this leads some people to see violence as acceptable. People may choose violent methods to solve a problem rather than exploring other options, such as discussion. Capella, a 16-year-old girl from Baltimore, Maryland, says:

" Many kids worship action stars like Van Damme and Vin Diesel. And if their heroes don't walk away, say sorry, or seek help, but shoot or fight first, then doesn't that say to impressionable kids that [this] is an okay way to act? "

POPULAR HEROES

5,000 12-year-olds in 23 countries were asked who they rate as role models:

Action hero	30% (boys)	21% (girls)
Pop star/musician	12% (boys)	27% (girls)
Religious leader	8%	
Military leader	7%	
Scientist or philosopher	6%	
Politician	3%	

UNESCO Global Media Violence Study, 1998

One of the best-known action-movie heroes, Jean-Claude Van Damme, in a scene from the 1994 film *Street Fighter*.

Just stories

Others, such as Barry, 17, from London, believe that young people are not so easily influenced by screen violence:

" Just because we like certain characters doesn't mean we follow everything they do. Most people know that it's only a story and that stories are twisted to include action, violence, and murder. The hero survives not because using violence was the right thing to do but because he's got to be in the sequel. **"**

CAN SCREEN VIOLENCE CAUSE SCHOOL SHOOTINGS?

The U.S. has been rocked by a series of school shootings, including in Columbine, Colorado (1999), and Red Lake, Minnesota (2005). In 1996, Thomas Hamilton killed 16 children and a teacher in Scotland, and Canada suffered a school murder in 1999. Is media violence a key cause?

Other causes of school shootings

Some people think that the media is merely a scapegoat. They blame the easy availability of guns or the unhappiness of the offender. Matt, 14, from Houston, Texas, believes:

❝ It's not the fault of guns, society, violent media, the parents, the school, the school district, the city, the state, or anyone else. Sometimes a person makes a decision to throw it all away and take out his rage on others. ❞

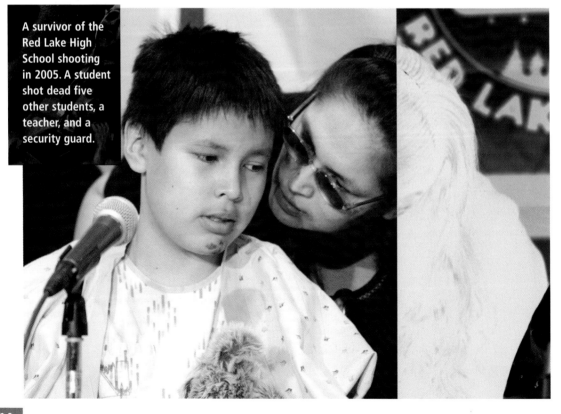

A survivor of the Red Lake High School shooting in 2005. A student shot dead five other students, a teacher, and a security guard.

In 2002, Robert Steinhaeuser shot dead 13 teachers, 2 students, and a police officer in his former school in Erfurt, Germany.

SCHOOL KILLERS

In a survey, members of the public answered the question: What is the main reason that kids commit violence like that which we saw at Columbine High School?

42% poor upbringing

26% media violence

14% peer pressure

4% genetic/biological tendencies

Public opinion survey, Pew Research Center, Washington, D.C., April 29, 2000

A major influence

Some people believe that certain violent movies or games have inspired school shooters to kill and have even given them practical tips. Columbine shooter Eric Harris, for instance, was a devoted player of the violent game *Doom* and named the shotgun he used after one of the game's characters.

"In America, violence is considered fun to kids—they play video games where they chop people's heads off and blood gushes, and it's fun, it's entertainment.... And I think that is in some of the psychology of these kids—this 'let's go out there and kill like on television.' "
Alvin Poussaint, Professor of Psychiatry at Harvard Medical School, *Salon*, 1998.

IS SCREEN VIOLENCE SOMETIMES VALID?

Some argue that screen violence can be essential—for example, to shock and warn people in an educational film or ad. Are certain uses of screen violence acceptable?

Telling it like it is

Some films, such as Oscar winners *Schindler's List* and *Platoon,* or acclaimed movies, such as *Osama* and *Hotel Rwanda,* deal with important issues such as racism and genocide or the realities of war. Some argue that for these films to be accurate and powerful, they must contain realistic violence. American teenage movie critic Roger Davidson says about World War II film *Saving Private Ryan*:

" For 20–plus minutes, the Normandy invasion and the taking of Omaha Beach are portrayed in accurately pulsating violence; it's not meant to be gratuitous but is supposed to shock and wake people up to the fact about what fighting a war...is really all about. "

Soldiers wade ashore surrounded by heavy gunfire in a scene from the film *Saving Private Ryan.*

"A September 2000 Federal Trade Commission report in the United States showed that 80 percent of R-rated movies [for those older than 18 only] and 70 percent of restricted video games with 'explicit content' warning labels were being marketed to children under 17."

Media Awareness Network, Canada, 2002.

Suspected criminals and terrorists are paraded on this Iraqi TV show. Some confess to their crimes or are identified by victims' families.

No real difference

Is there a genuine difference between violence that is necessary for a story and violence that is gratuitous—included just to thrill? Felix, 15, from Lyons, France, doubts it:

❝ Violence—artistically necessary? Oh, come on! Couldn't they have made it without the violence? Of course they could. They mean it is necessary so that they make money by people going to see it. And anyway, who decides whether violence is okay or not okay? Everyone has a different opinion. ❞

IS CENSORSHIP JUSTIFIED?

Censorship is an attempt to limit or prevent the exchange of information. It can be used by a government to prevent criticism and also to protect society from material considered offensive or harmful. Is censorship a force for good?

A useful tool

In Australia, the video games *Manhunt* and *Grand Theft Auto III* have been banned from sale because of their graphic violent content. Capella, 16, from Baltimore, thinks censorship is useful:

❝ What is worse—a film not being seen by people or someone losing their life because of someone inspired by violent movies and games? ❞

In 2004, *Manhunt* was taken off the shelves of many UK stores after it was claimed that the game inspired 17-year-old Warren Leblanc to kill 14-year-old Stefan Pakeerah in Leicester, England.

U.S. Senator Joseph I. Lieberman helped sponsor the V-Chip law. Here, he gives a talk about the V-Chip with video conference links to many schools.

Censorship can be electronic as well. The V-Chip is a computer chip that has been installed in new televisions in the U.S. since 2000. Parents use a rating system to set which programs they will allow their children to watch. The V-Chip blocks all other programs.

Protecting free speech and expression

Free speech is the right for people to communicate any opinion without interference or punishment. In some countries, such as the U.S., the right to free speech and expression is part of the constitution. Many argue that by censoring media content because it is violent, people are denied their rights.

The American Booksellers Foundation for Free Expression explains why its members believe violence in books should not be censored. This could also apply to screen violence:

● **censorship won't solve the root causes of violence in society**

● **deciding what is "acceptable" content is a subjective exercise**

● **many of the plays, books, and films banned in the past are considered classics today**

● **it's up to individuals and not governments to decide what's appropriate for them and their children.**

Media Awareness Network Web site, Canada, 2005.

SHOULD THE MEDIA DO MORE?

Media companies sometimes cut violent scenes in their programs and print warnings on the packaging. But should they produce less violent material in the first place?

The Peaceoholics campaign group demonstrates outside the offices of the makers of the violent computer game *Grand Theft Auto: San Andreas*.

Money matters

By including violence in their products, some media companies have found that they can sell their products more easily and make more money. The media should be more responsible, argues U.S. psychologist Joanne Cantor:

❝ They say that it's up to parents, not the media, to raise their children. But they make harmful products.... They market them to children too young to use them safely, and they try to keep parents in the dark about their effects. ❞

Actress Sarah Michelle Gellar playing the role of Buffy Summers in the hit TV show *Buffy the Vampire Slayer*.

Not up to us

Sarah Michelle Gellar, star of *Buffy the Vampire Slayer*, is one of many in the media industry who think that it is not their job to teach people how to act in society:

❝ I've always felt that, as an entertainer, my job is to tell a story and make people feel things, which may not always mean taking the moral high ground. If a teenager can't discern right from wrong or fiction from reality, I'm pretty confident that it has little to do with whether he or she watches Buffy or plays aggressive video games. It's more to do with the fact that society has failed to teach him or her. ❞

U.S. VIEWERS SURVEYED

In a survey of American viewers:

68% believe the entertainment industry has lost touch with viewers' moral standards.

75% believe the entertainment industry needs to greatly reduce violence in its content.

66% believe there is too much violence on TV.

53% believe there should be stricter controls on TV broadcasts of sex and violence.

TIME *magazine survey, March 2005*

In many countries, films, computer games, and TV shows have ratings or warnings. Certain films are not for children at all, while some may be viewed if the child is with an adult. Does this system work?

Clear warnings?

Ratings can give parents a clear warning about unsuitable content. Hannan, 13, from Newcastle, England, thinks that the authorities could go farther:

" Many children are learning about things they're too young to know about from watching too much TV and unsuitable TV shows. I think that not only should TV shows have ratings, but that adult channels should be viewed only by adults entering a password. "

Two young teenage girls watch a hard-hitting show about domestic violence featuring graphic and realistic violent acts.

Many children watch shows late at night in their own rooms without their parents knowing what they are viewing.

Tempting teens?

Rating systems and warnings will work only if people use them strictly, though. Gerry, 15, from Brisbane, Australia, believes that rating systems act as an advertisement, not a warning to teens, and are easy to get around:

❝ As soon as you see an 'R' rating for a movie, game, or show, you want to watch it because it has something in it you shouldn't see. Getting ahold of a copy is a no-brainer. There's always someone whose folks will tape it or burn it. If it's a new movie, you can wait until it's for rent and say, 'It's for my dad.' No one checks. Or you can sneak into a theater, easy. ❞

"The warning acts as an advertisement, in a sense, for the coming program, inducing interest in the adolescent viewer to watch the program."

Jay Handelman and Michael Parent, University of Western Ontario, Canada, 1997.

IS IT PARENTS' RESPONSIBILITY?

Parents complain about screen violence and the companies that produce it. Yet many of them let children watch what they like or don't monitor their viewing carefully. Are parents doing enough to protect their children?

Parents to blame?

Rachel, 14, from Norfolk, England, has had enough of parents blaming screen violence for their children's behavior:

" I'm sick and tired of people saying that what we watch can make us violent or misbehave. What we watch is not who we are! And if children go out and misbehave, shouldn't their parents have taught them better? I think bad parents use this as an excuse to ignore the real issues about their child and ignore their responsibilities. "

Parents who watch TV with their children are able to explain troubling images. They can switch channels if a show becomes too violent or disturbing.

Some families strive to replace screen entertainment with outdoor pursuits such as skiing. But many families do not have such opportunities.

A hard task

However, it's not that easy for parents because there are so many different media for them to monitor. Many teens have access to portable DVD players, TVs, or their own computer. Even if parents are strict at home, they have no control when their children are at friends' houses. British parent Tom Kemp believes that monitoring children is an almost impossible task:

CHILDREN WITH TVS IN BEDROOM

UK (under 5)	36%
U.S. (under 6)	43%
UK (under 16)	52%
U.S. (under 18)	68%

Independent Television Commission, 2001; Kaiser Family Foundation, 2003

❝ Even if there were no such thing as video recorders, even if children did not have television sets in their own rooms, there would be only one way to ensure that children saw nothing unsuitable on television and that would be to broadcast nothing unsuitable for them, at any hour of the day or night. ❞

CONCLUSION

Violence on our screens is a complex issue with strong opinions on different sides. Should governments and the media industry decide what to do, or can individuals make a difference?

Everyone's responsibility

Kerri, a teen from Massachusetts, believes that reducing screen violence should be a priority:

" If violence is constantly portrayed on television and sometimes even glorified, it becomes an integrated part of society.... Perhaps by lessening the number of violent occurrences portrayed on TV, the way to a more peaceful society can be begun. "

Damon Dash is presented with an award for his work with SHiNE (Seeking Harmony in Neighborhoods Everyday). The organization works toward ending youth violence.

2007 SHiNE HONOREE
DAMON DASH

Protestors against guns campaign outside the 2004 national convention of the National Rifle Association (NRA) in the U.S.

Individual choice

Others think that it is up to individuals to watch what they like. Steve, 17, from Birmingham, England, says:

❝ I just don't see what all the fuss is about. If you don't like watching violence, read the TV guide or the movie reviews and don't watch. If violence comes on-screen, turn it off. I think people should have the choice. Even if I felt differently, there's nothing I could do against big business anyway. ❞

Stand up and be counted

However, Danielle Shimotakahara from Oregon has proved that individuals can make a difference. At age 13, she started the Cool-No-Violence Peace Project, a successful campaign to find nonviolent video games to replace violent games found in businesses and places open to young children.

"I would tell other young people that if you feel something needs to be changed to make society safer and better, you can do it…. Don't think just because you are young, people won't listen to you."

Danielle Shimotakahara, Testimony to U.S. Senate, 2000.

TIMELINE

1907   Chief Secretary of the Australian state of Victoria bans screenings of the film *The Kelly Gang*.

1912   The British Board of Film Censors is formed.

1965   The National Viewers and Listeners Association is formed in the UK.

1972   In the UK, a Nationwide Petition for Public Decency, mainly in response to screen violence, attracts one and a half million signatures.

1976–80 The satellite TV industry starts up in the U.S.

1978   The U.S. Supreme Court holds that the government can constitutionally regulate indecent broadcasts.

1981   In the U.S., Charles Rocket, the "Weekend Update" anchor on *Saturday Night Live*, swears on TV and is fired.

1984   The British government outlaws "video nasties"—films depicting extreme horror, mutilation, and violence.

1984   The Video Recordings Act allows the British Board of Film Censors to give ratings to videos.

1988   The Australian Office of Film and Literature Classification (OFLC) begins to identify media products that children should not be permitted to see.

1989   At a school in Montreal, Canada, 14 female students are gunned down.

1991   The Motion Picture Association in the U.S. says that only 16 percent of American movies are suitable for children under 13.

1991   *Terminator 2* demonstrates a new type of ultra-realistic computer special effects called morphing.

1993   *NYPD Blue*, network television's first R-rated series, is launched in the U.S.

1994   Toddler Jamie Bulger is abducted and killed by two 10-year-old boys, who claimed they were inspired to kill by horror films.

1994   The film *Natural Born Killers* is released. Containing more than 50 murders, it was later claimed to have inspired several killings.

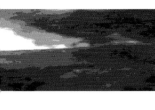

1995	U.S. law makes it compulsory to install a V-Chip in all new TV sets more than 13 inches (33 cm) in size.
1996	The Internet has 45 million users.
1996	A study by the American Psychological Association links violence on television with aggressive behavior, especially in children.
1996	Thomas Hamilton kills 16 children and one teacher and wounds 10 others at Dunblane Primary School in Scotland before committing suicide.
1997	DVDs go on sale to the public.
1997	Streaming audio and video are available on the Internet.
1997	Michael Carneal, 14, kills three students and wounds five at Heath High School, Kentucky.
1998	An 11-year-old kills 5 people and wounds 10 at Westside Middle School in Jonesboro, Arkansas.
1999	The Columbine High School shooting leaves the 2 teenage killers, 12 students, and 1 teacher dead, as well as 23 wounded.
2001	An American college student dies while imitating a dangerous stunt from the TV show *Jackass*.
2001	For the first time, Americans spend more on electronic games than on movie tickets.
2002	The lawsuit brought by parents of victims of the Columbine school shootings against violent video game makers is dropped.
2002	Robert Steinhaeuser, 19, kills 13 teachers, 2 students, and 1 policeman and wounds 10 people at a secondary school in Erfurt, Germany.
2003	Norway's national film board lifts a ban on more than 100 movies, including *Predator 2, Commando,* and *On Deadly Ground*.
2005	Jeff Weise, 16, kills 9 people before taking his own life in Red Lake, Minnesota.
2005	The Family Entertainment and Copyright Act is introduced into the U.S. Congress. It is designed to make new technology available to shield children from unwanted violence and other offensive material in movies.

GLOSSARY

abuse Wrong use, mistreatment, or taking advantage of someone.

adolescent A young person who has undergone puberty but who has not reached full maturity.

aggressive Angry and unfriendly; seeming likely to use violence.

censorship The act of changing or stopping information that is communicated between a sender and a receiver.

copycat violence An act of violence that mimics a previous act of violence.

counseling Advice and support to help people deal with personal problems.

desensitize To make someone less sensitive to violence through frequent and repeated viewing of it.

fictional Not real; made up by a writer, filmmaker, or artist.

free speech The right to express or listen to any opinion in public without being pressured or punished by the authorities.

gratuitous Unnecessary, unjustified, and often extreme.

lawsuit A claim or complaint about a person or organization made in a court of law.

mass media One of the ways in which information can be communicated publicly to a large audience, such as film, TV, or the Internet.

ratings The grading of films, video games, and TV shows into different classes based on their content and the age of the viewers that should be permitted access to them.

role model A person whom someone admires and whose behavior he or she tries to copy.

street children Children who have run away from home or been left or orphaned, and who survive by living on the streets.

V-Chip A computer chip installed in a television to allow the user to control the display of certain programs, especially those with high sexual or violent content.

victim A person subjected to pain, abuse, suffering, or death.

vulnerable Being especially at risk.

RESOURCES

Books

Carter, Cynthia, and C. Kay Weaver.
Violence and the Media. Philadelphia,
Penn.: Open University Press, 2003.
An introduction to media violence and its
potential influence on audiences.

Gelletly, LeeAnne. *Violence in the
Media*. San Diego: Lucent Books, 2005.
Examines whether or not real-life violence is
caused by violence in the media.

Lang, Susan. *Censorship*. New York:
Franklin Watts, 1993.
Presents an overview of a wide range of issues
relating to First Amendment rights.

Steele, Philip. *Censorship*. New York: New
Discovery Books, 1992.
Provides historical overviews, along with
present-day information, on the controversial
topic of censorship.

Steins, Richard. *Censorship: How Does
it Conflict with Freedom?* New York:
Twenty-first Century Books, 1995.
Presents a well-rounded, unbiased discussion
of censorship and encourages readers to form
their own conclusions.

Web sites

http://www.media-awareness.ca/english/
issues/violence/index.cfm
A Canadian Web site that examines many
issues surrounding violence and its portrayal
in the media.

http://www.movie-ratings.net/index.shtml
A useful Web site explaining the different
movie rating systems in a number of countries,
including the UK, Australia, and the U.S.

http://www.mpaa.org
Web site of the Motion Picture Association of
America (MPAA).

http://www.youngmedia.org.au
An Australian Web site with discussions,
reports, and advice on handling media violence.

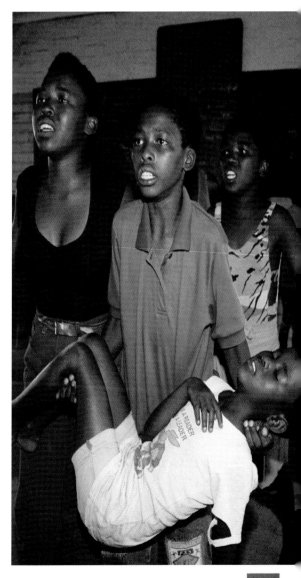

INDEX